WALKS AROUND WINDERMERE

10 WALKS UNDER 6 MILES

DALESMAN

Dalesman Publishing Company Ltd
Stable Courtyard, Broughton Hall,
Skipton, North Yorkshire BD23 3AE

First Edition 1997
Reprinted 1998

Text © Robert Gambles

Illustrations © Christine Isherwood:
p5 Bank Barn, Townend; p10 celandines; p14 heron; p17 red squirrel;
p21 yellow irises; p26 Windermere from Rosthwaite; p31 wild daffodils

Cover: Leaving Waterhead, Windermere, by R Dixon

A British Library Cataloguing in Publication record
is available for this book

ISBN 1 85568 116 1

Printed by Amadeus Press, Huddersfield

Contents

Introduction

England's longest lake, Windermere, is the central feature of this southern area of the Lake District. All but one of these ten walks lie within one mile of the lakeshore and one of the many pleasures to look forward to is the sudden glimpses of the water shining through the trees or a fine view along the lake from more open ground. For this is a landscape of wooded hills where many small tarns nestle in the hollows and tempting rocky knolls offer spectacular vistas of Lakeland's highest fells. Rarely is one far away from the sound of running water as innumerable becks tumble their way down from the heights and into the lake below. Open heathlands are bright with spring flowers, autumn heather or ablaze with gorse at all times. Lush meadowlands surround ancient farmsteads and white stone-built cottages, set in tiny gardens, stand out sharp and clear against the green, while sweeping lawns and giant trees adorn the grounds of Victorian residences.

This is not wilderness country. There are no steep crags or cloud-capped peaks to overawe this gentle landscape. Indeed, Windermere may be described as a great pond set in a huge garden where the labours of Man have overlaid the hand of Nature to create a different version of natural beauty. A keen eye will see the works of Man at every stage along these walks. Houses, farms and churches and the age-old ferry are obvious examples; perhaps of greater interest are those features created to produce the food and goods Man needed in order to survive in earlier times. Hidden in the woods are the remains of bobbin mills, lime kilns, charcoal-burning pitsteads, iron forges, smelting furnaces, mill-races and dams. More visible are packhorse bridges and ancient stiles on once-busy tracks and paths, the old gateposts laboriously chiselled and the miles of skilfully built drystone walls.

It is, above all, the lake which dominates the scene. More than ten miles long and 220 feet deep but never more than half a mile wide, it seems, as Wordsworth described it, "like a vast river, stretching in the sun" and dotted with islands bearing romantic names such as Ling Holme, Belle Isle and Lily of the Valley. Windermere and the gentle, picturesque countryside around it, is the idyllic setting for the stories of Beatrix Potter and the adventures of Arthur Ransome's *'Swallows and Amazons'*.

All this may be discovered and enjoyed on these easy walks for people of all ages.

Brockhole

Length of walk: 3¹/₂ miles.
Start/finish: Brockhole National Park Visitor Centre on A591 road, two miles north of Windermere.
Terrain: Mostly on good tracks or footpaths, a few rough sections. Care needed in crossing A591 to and from Brockhole at the beginning and end of the walk.

This walk is almost entirely on ancient trackways and visits the National Trust property at Townend in the historic village of Troutbeck. There is a wealth of plant life to be seen as well as a variety of birds and some fine views over the Troutbeck valley and Windermere. The National Park Visitor Centre at Brockhole is housed in a mansion built almost 100 years ago for a Manchester businessman, William Henry Gaddum, and it is situated in extensive grounds with beautiful gardens and walks through woodland and by the lakeshore. There are changing exhibitions, illustrated lectures, a well-stocked information shop and a pleasant cafeteria. A popular children's play-area is in the grounds. There is a large car park.

The walk starts at the entrance to Brockhole by the A591. Cross the road with great care to a bridleway sign almost directly opposite. This leads into Mirk Lane, at first the driveway to Merewood Cottages and Merewood House which are passed on the left. After Wood Farm – about 250m further on – the 'lane' becomes a narrow path through a wooded area before once again opening out as a broad track, a pleasant section which ends in about 350m at the junction with Holbeck Lane.

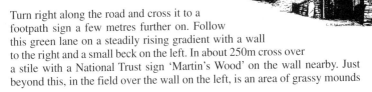

Turn right along the road and cross it to a footpath sign a few metres further on. Follow this green lane on a steadily rising gradient with a wall to the right and a small beck on the left. In about 250m cross over a stile with a National Trust sign 'Martin's Wood' on the wall nearby. Just beyond this, in the field over the wall on the left, is an area of grassy mounds

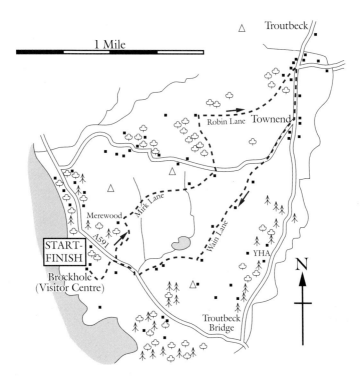

and hollows marking the site of an ancient British settlement, formerly referred to as the 'castle', a name preserved in the beck below – Castle Dyke.

Continue forward for a short distance to cross another stile to join a wide track. Turn right here for a few metres only and at the T-junction turn right again into Robin Lane. A large square cairn high above this junction of lanes has a splendid view and may be reached by a stone stile over the wall by the corner. Robin Lane is an ancient trackway connecting Troutbeck and Ambleside and is thought to be the route of the Roman Road from the fort at Ambleside to High Street and on to Penrith. It is good, easy walking with a seat situated at another junction further on from which to enjoy the spectacular view over Lake Windermere.

Continue ahead along Robin Lane for another 500m. As the lane descends an impressive range of peaks appears through the trees on the left: Yoke, Ill Bell and Froswick with High Street beyond. Look for a bridleway sign by a large

6

ash tree on the right. This is a short link down to the Troutbeck road. It is rather a gloomy path so beware of a deep channel on the left-hand side. On reaching the road notice a cottage on the right – 'Glenside' – which is very much older than it looks. Turn right along the road and in approximately 150m pass by Townend House on the right and a fine example of a Lakeland bank barn opposite.

Bank barns are so called because they are built on the contours of a bank or hill-slope, on the lower side of the barns is an entrance to a cow-shed or stable while on the upper level a ramp gives access to a large hayloft. They are particularly associated with the Lake District and Scandinavia. The barn at Troutbeck is probably unique in having two wings which may have been accommodation for farm workers, and a so-called 'spinning gallery'. It bears the date 1666.

Just beyond the barn take the right fork in the road. The entrance to Townend is less than 50m further on. Townend is a fine example of a prosperous Lakeland yeoman's house from the early 17th century. It has mullioned windows and large round chimneys and its rooms are richly panelled with Jacobean oak and furnished with period cupboards, beds, chests and cradles and many fascinating implements and utensils. The Brownes lived here from 1626, when the house was built, until 1943. The house is open from the beginning of April until the end of October, Tuesdays to Fridays, Sundays and Bank Holiday Mondays: 1-5pm.

From Townend continue along the road and in about 400m leave the road at a bridleway sign on the left. This is Wain Lane, an old road linking Troutbeck with Windermere. It is now a rough track bounded by stone walls and hedges and with a number of bank barns and field barns along the way. The first barn is near the start of the lane on the right: it is dated 1695 and is still in use. Look out for others on the way. Wain Lane is a happy hunting ground for the botanist. Here are found many mosses, ferns and lichens, a remarkable assortment of fungi, at least ten tree species, and more than 50 flowering plants from the early spring celandines to the late contrary ivy which flowers in late autumn.

Near the end of the lane, which is just under one mile in length, is a man-made tarn near Middlerigg, an 18th century country house. The tarn itself is probably a 20th century addition to the landscape as it does not appear on old maps. Herons, swans, various ducks and coots are often seen here. On reaching the road, cross with great care to the footpath on the other side. Turn right to walk the 250m back to Brockhole.

Wray Castle

Length of walk: 4 miles.
Start/finish: Wray Castle on the Western shore of Windermere near the northern end of the lake. Take a minor road off the B5286 Clappersgate to Hawkshead road, signposted 'Wray Castle'. There are spaces for a few cars near the gateway to the castle or it may be possible to find a space in the car parks situated behind the castle. Terrain: Meadow and woodland paths are all fairly easy walking but the short climb to the summit of Latterbarrow is quite steep. A walk of great variety and splendid views: a real gem.

The walk starts and finishes at Wray Castle or alternatively from the castle gateway. Wray Castle is a grey, stone, gothic structure built in 1840 for James Dawson, a Liverpool surgeon. It is massive and slightly absurd in a Lakeland setting, and even when it was built it was described as 'a great foolish toy'. It is now used as a telecommunications centre. The grounds but not the castle are open to the public (National Trust).

From the castle car park return to the gateway along the drive with a fine view of the Langdale Pikes. Turn left at the gateway and walk along the road for 250m to a footpath sign on the right marked with a yellow arrow. Follow this path, which has black waymark arrows, for 175m, to a footbridge over a beck. Note that the stones of the bridge were originally ancient fence posts with square holes chiselled out of them for the fence poles.

Continue along the path through a kissing gate and across a field with a beck running alongside. Cross over two stiles noting the large stone slabs and also the special dog-stile which will appear in almost all the stiles on this walk. There is now a good view of Blelham Tarn over to the right as you follow the black arrows all the way to a gate at the entrance to a farm.

Blelham Tarn and the surrounding bog are a National Nature Reserve of special interest to environmental scientists. The unusual variety of habitats here has encouraged a rich wildlife and many types of plant communities. The tarn was at one time a valuable fishery belonging to the monks of Furness Abbey. Beyond the farm continue straight ahead on a macadam road for about 100m

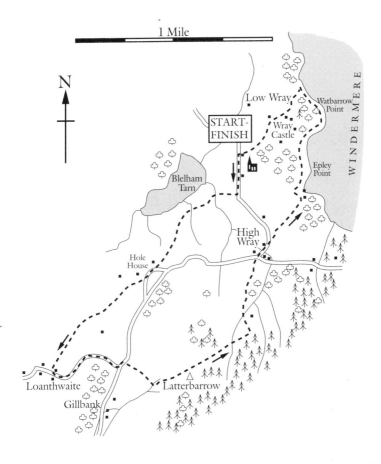

and then turn right (footpath sign) towards Tock How. In less than 50m turn left by a footpath sign to Loanthwaite and through a gate on to a path rising gently to a splendid viewpoint with Blelham Tarn and Lake Windermere in the foreground and a wide panorama of the Lakeland fells beyond.

Follow the black arrows down to a double stile and just beyond this the path turns sharply to the left across the meadows and proceeds through several gates to the farm at Loanthwaite Lane. Turn left along the lane and pass between its wide hedgerows enjoying the wild flowers and the distant spectacle of the sharp ridges of Crinkle Crags and Bowfell. Turn left again at the T-junction and in about 100m look for the sign to Latterbarrow on the right. Follow the main track forward as it rises gently at first and soon enters an area of woodland.

Many alder trees will be seen alongside the path. These trees flourish in conditions which are too damp for many other species. The wood of the alder is resistant to damp and is also easy to use, so for many centuries it was in great demand for the making of clogs. In the spring, look for the attractive catkins and in the autumn and winter for the small, hard cones, green at first and then almost black. In a short distance a wide grassy path rises steeply on the left and leads directly to the summit of Latterbarrow with its impressive cairn. Latterbarrow is 244m (803ft) in height and its delightful summit plateau is a pleasant place to rest awhile to enjoy the outstanding views of the Lakeland fells, the Howgill fells, the Duddon Estuary and the Pennines.

To begin the descent from Latterbarrow follow the path from the cairn leading directly towards Lake Windermere. It is not a difficult path but care is advisable after wet weather. Continue down to a wall and a stile and go forward through woods of birch and oak, following the arrows, down to a gate by a forest road. Turn left along this track, pass by the National Trust Basecamp, and join the road at the village of High Wray.

Turn right and just beyond a minor road signposted to the Ferry and by a house called 'The Cottage' take a footpath on the right signposted 'To the Lake'. A stone stile almost immediately on the left leads to a field path which goes beside a wall or fence to a kissing gate and then straight down to the lakeshore at High Wray Bay.

Turn left to follow the path by the lake passing through two gates. Very shortly after the latter look for a gate by a National Trust sign on the right. From here continue along the shore path, eventually climbing a grassy slope to enter the castle woods. The path soon swings round to skirt the edge of the woods and returns to the castle and the start of the walk.

Orrest Head

Length of walk: 3 miles.
Start/finish: The Tourist Information Centre near Windermere Station.
Terrain: A steady climb to the summit, an easy descent, woodland paths, half a mile downhill on a fairly quiet road.

The walk to Orrest Head is probably – and deservedly – the most popular walk from Windermere. The reward for so little effort is a remarkable panorama along the length of the lake and to the mountain peaks of central Lakeland.

A signpost on the opposite side of the A591 from the Tourist Office marks the beginning of the path to Orrest Head. It begins as a tarmac lane. Ignore a sign which soon appears on the left – 'A592 Troutbeck Road' – and continue uphill on the tarmac through a number of sweeping bends. When the surfaced road ends follow the track upward through the woodland to a signpost by a tangle of tree roots by a wall. Turn right here along a path lined with some very fine trees, a welcome seat and a good view. This is an easy level stretch of the route and leads to a kissing gate in the wall on the left which has a memorial plaque recording the gift of Orrest Head for public enjoyment.

Through the gate the summit is only a few paces away with a variety of seats and a view-finder: a place to pause and admire the magnificent view. It is difficult to believe that here one is no more than 784ft (238m) above sea level. On a clear day one can see the highest peaks in the Lake District, the distant line of the Pennines, most of Windermere and the wooded heights beyond it, and the waters of Morecambe Bay. From the summit take the grassy path to the north down towards a narrow road. This path can be quite wet in some hollows after heavy rain. The road is joined at a stile opposite Causeway Farm, a 17th century homestead named after the Roman road – or 'causeway' – from Kendal to Ambleside which ran across the nearby fields.

Causeway Farm is a typical Lakeland farm with a long tradition of sheep-rearing. The earliest farmers here were probably familiar with the ancient system of sheep-counting once used throughout the Lake District and which may have had its origins in the days of the Celtic tribes who inhabited the area more than a thousand years ago. Sheep were counted in units of 20 and when that number was reached the shepherd raised one finger. Five fingers represented

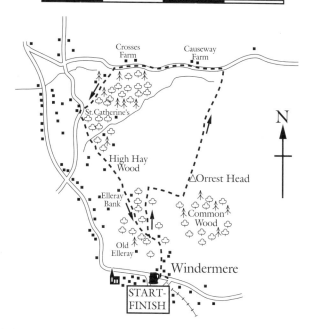

1 Mile

Crosses Farm

Causeway Farm

St.Catherine's

High Hay Wood

△Orrest Head

N

Elleray Bank

Common Wood

Old Elleray

Windermere

START-FINISH

100 sheep and this was registered by placing a pebble in a pocket. Each valley had a variant of the numbers used but one of the easiest to learn is that used in Borrowdale. Try it!:

1 Yan, 2 Tyan, 3 Tethera, 4 Methera, 5 Pimp,
6 Sethera, 7 Lethera, 8 Hovera, 9 Dovera, 10 Dick,
11 Yan-a-dick, Tyan-a-dick, 13 Tethera-dick, 14 Methera-dick, 15 Bumfit,
16 Yan-a-bumfit, 17 Tyan-a-bumfit, 18 Tethera-bumfit, 19 Methera-bumfit, 20
Giggot.

Turn left along the road and continue for about half a mile to the bottom of a hill. Just before the main road is reached look for a metal gate on the left with a footpath sign. Go through this on to a track and walk straight ahead across the field to a gate and into woodland. Cross a footbridge and continue along the clear path passing by a number of impressive trees and colourful gardens to return to the tarmac road near the start of the walk. Orrest Head was at one time the residence of an eccentric named Josiah Brown who was renowned for his hospitality to beggars and for keeping a bull on which he rode about the district, challenging other bulls he met on the way.

Biskey Howe

Length of walk: 4¹/₄ miles.
Start/finish: St Martin's Church in Bowness-on-Windermere. There are several car parks nearby.
Terrain: A steady climb out of Bowness is followed by easy to moderate walking and a short, steep climb to the summit of Brant Fell. Road walking in Bowness is on quiet side roads; a 150m section of main road later on needs special care.

From St Martin's Church walk for a short distance to the mini-roundabout and about 100m up the hill beyond this turn right into Helm Road. This climbs steadily for 500m passing on the way the Windermere Hydro Hotel, and at the top on the left hand side is the fine viewpoint of Biskey Howe – look for the sign.

Biskey Howe is a splendid rocky hilltop with glorious views over the lake and the surrounding woods and to many of the highest Lakeland peaks. There are several seats and a useful view-finder to pinpoint the various fell-tops. Return to the road from the viewpoint and go through a gateway almost immediately opposite: do not be deterred by the 'Private Road' sign, this is a public footpath. A 'cross-roads' just beyond this has several footpath signs: follow the route to Post Knott. When the Tarmac road swings to the left go straight ahead on an unsurfaced track to a kissing gate with a National Trust signpost, 'Post Knott'.

Continue forward to a gateway where the Dales Way crosses this track – signposted. Turn left here and follow the path up the field alongside the wall and through a gate to cross the drive by Brantfell Farm. Follow the Dales Way sign forward to a kissing gate with yellow arrow waymarks. Take the path which bears to the left across the fields. The route is waymarked through two more gates and then straight ahead crossing the tarmac drive by several giant sequoia trees. Beyond the kissing gate the path continues across another field, bears left at the corner of a wall to reach another gate and the drive to Helm Farm.

Go straight ahead to a kissing gate and along a narrow path with a wire fence on the right-hand side. Cross over a small stone stile and bear right as the path continues alongside the gardens of an estate of modern houses.

In 200m at a cluster of footpath signs, all of which point to Windermere, turn very sharply to the right to take the path fairly steeply up to a wall where it bears left to pass through a gate beside a house. Continue forward to reach an iron gate giving access to a tarmac lane. Turn right along the lane for 200m, and take the first turning to the left and walk down to a cottage on the left which has an interesting display of topiary work. Opposite the cottage is a footpath sign by a gate leading into a field. Follow the path until it meets a wide track. Turn right along this track and follow it for the next three-quarters of a mile, ignoring a Dales Way fork to the left and passing through several gates and crossing several becks.

After the final gate the track becomes a tarmac lane by a few houses and shortly joins a busy road. A small tarn just before this is often frequented by various ducks, herons and swans. Turn right along the road for 150m and keep close to the right-hand verge: a few minutes of care and alertness will bring you safely to a right turn by a red letter box. Proceed along this quiet lane for 200m. Just before a group of white cottages a large, blue public footpath sign indicates a turn to the left. Pass through a gate and turn immediately right along a hedge down the field to a cluster of three kissing gates by a large oak tree. Go through all these and then follow the waymark posts with yellow arrows over a slight rise and through a small grove of oak trees and down to a kissing gate. The path continues straight ahead across a field bright with gorse to another gate by a narrow lane. Cross over to a footpath sign 'Dales Way' and go down the next field alongside a hedge to a farm driveway.

Cross straight over to follow the waymarks through another gate into a small field. Where the path forks take the left branch to a kissing gate in the wall. Just beyond this, turn right for a few metres along a driveway before bearing left by a Dales Way signpost. An iron gate gives access to a slightly raised path across a field. All the land here forms part of the Matson Ground Estate.

From the iron gate go forward to a gate at the corner of the wall, turn left and pass through another gate to rejoin the outward path by the drive way near Brantfell Farm. Cross over the drive and go straight ahead and in a few metres,

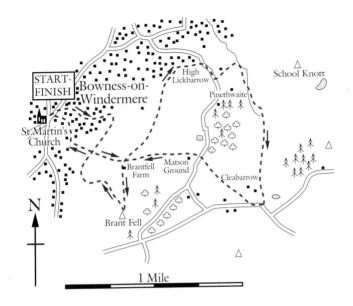

immediately on the other side of a gate, turn left up a short flight of stone steps (footpath sign) which mark the beginning of the path up to the top of Brant Fell.

Follow the fence for a few metres and then the path bears right up the grassy slope to a group of trees. The arrows lead the way to a stone stile over a wall. Immediately on the other side paths are signposted to both left and right. Ignore these and go straight ahead on a permissive path which makes a bee-line for the summit of the fell. The path is clear but several large cairns help to mark the way.

Brant Fell boasts a height of only 629ft (191m) but it enjoys a spectacular view which many a much higher peak might envy. The summit area is a delightful place of grassy sward, knolls and rock faces, a superb spot for play and picnics. The iron rods embedded in the rock are all that remains of a summer house.

Begin the descent by the same route as the ascent but near to a fenced plantation bear left by a large cairn and go down to a ladder stile over the wall at the far corner. Over the stile follow the path bearing right to the promontory of Post Knott with its famous prospect over Windermere – one of Lakeland's best-known viewpoints. Continue forward through a kissing gate into a woodland. Bear left and follow a broad track through the wood – note the stone seats on the way. At a gateway where the Dales Way crosses the drive turn left and follow the path fairly steeply down the field.

Part way down the hill is a stone structure with a useful seat. This marks the end of the Dales Way which, a notice informs us, began in Ilkley 81 miles away. A gate at the bottom of the hill leads to the road back to Bowness. To return to the starting point of the walk turn right into Langrigge Road shortly after joining the tarmac. This quiet and 'traffic-calmed' residential road emerges at the foot of Helm Road. Turn left for St. Martin's Church.

Beatrix Potter Walk

Length of walk: 5 miles.
Start/finish: Windermere Ferry. Car Park at Ferry Nab near the Bowness Pier. Turn right out of the car park. The pier is 200m away at the end of the road.
Terrain: There are a few hills to climb but in general the route is not too strenuous and passes through pleasant meadows and woodlands and along sections of fairly quiet country lanes.

The walk includes a visit to Beatrix Potter's cottage at Hill Top where she wrote and illustrated many of her famous Peter Rabbit books. Allow an extra hour for a visit to Hill Top which is a National Trust property open 11a.m. to 5p.m. from April to November 1 except on Thursdays and Fridays.

Cross by the ferry, walk along the road for about 200m and look for a gate with a footpath sign on the right-hand side almost opposite the main entrance to the Freshwater Ecology Institute. Follow this path along the edge of the water to a gate by the lakeshore road. Turn left and in about 100m, just on the bend of the ferry road, go through a gap in the wall on the right with a National Trust sign 'To Near Sawrey and Hill Top'. Walk up the path to a ruined building known as 'The Station'.

Guidebook writers of the 18th and 19th centuries drew the attention of visitors to certain prominent viewpoints which they called 'stations'. These may be found in most parts of the Lake District. This station overlooking Windermere belonged to the Ferry Hotel (now Ferry House) and visitors could sit here in comfort to admire the view.

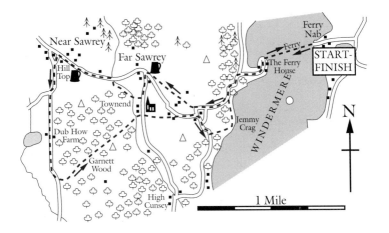

From the station descend by way of the paved and stepped pathway. Turn right at the bottom by a white post: a small National Trust car park is a few metres away among the trees. Leave the car park by the permissive path signed 'National Trust. Footpath to Near Sawrey and Hill Top'. The path goes alongside woodland frequented by red squirrels to a gate at the far end. Here cross the road with care to join a continuation of the path on the opposite side. At the end, near the top of the hill, walk along the roadside for a short distance to a bend where a track on the right is signed 'Public Footpath. Far Sawrey'. Cross the road and follow this. At the top of a rise go through a kissing gate, noting the interesting growth of ferns in and on the wall, and proceed to another ancient iron kissing gate. Join the tarmac lane; keep straight ahead on to a narrow path which goes down to meet the road into Far Sawrey by the Sawrey Hotel and the 'Claife Crier' inn.

The name 'Crier of Claife' refers to a dreadful spectre reputed to haunt the nearby Claife Heights. The story goes that one stormy night more than 300 years ago the ferryman heard a voice calling for the ferry. He crossed the lake alone to answer the call but returned alone, white-haired and terrified, and died two days later. It was believed that he had met the ghost of a monk from Furness Abbey who had haunted the heights for many years, crying out his despair at his rejection by a woman he loved. The ghost was exorcised and confined forever to the quarry marked on the map 'Crier of Claife'.

Continue on the road past the Hotel and the Claife Crier and very shortly turn left on a minor road by the Sawrey Stores (shop and post office). Walk through the village and just before reaching the church take a footpath on the right through a kissing gate (footpath sign). Follow the path across the fields to another kissing gate and immediately turn sharp left on a permissive path signed to 'Near Sawrey and Hill Top'. The path eventually goes through a gate on to the road. Go left and the entrance to Hill Top cottage is only a short distance away.

This 17th century cottage, now preserved by the National Trust, was where Beatrix Potter wrote and painted. It is seen today very much as she left it. The cottage garden is illustrated in *The Tale of Tom Kitten*; the exterior appears in the drawings for *The Tale of Pigling Bland* and *The Tale of Jemima Puddleduck*; the hall and staircase will be recognisable from *The Tale of Samuel Whiskers*. In and around the village are the sites of many other illustrations from her stories. Guided walks are available from Hill Top to many of these points of interest.

Continue along the road towards Hawkshead and take the first turning left into a minor road signed to 'Lakeside' and 'YHA'. At the fork in the road (shown in *Pigling Bland*) keep left. In just under half a mile look for a footpath on the left going into woodland and signed to 'Far Sawrey'. Go over two stiles and climb fairly steeply through the wood along a clear path.

This is a typical mixed Lakeland broadleaved woodland of oak, ash, birch, alder, hazel, lime, crab apple, sallow, yew, hawthorn, blackthorn and rowan. Shrubs include bramble, wild rose, raspberry and broom. The path levels at the top of the wood where a stile leads into a field. Aim for the distant gate, go over the stile by it and head for the next gate. Go straight ahead along a terraced footpath to reach a kissing gate by the roadside.

Turn left on the road and then almost immediately turn right through a kissing gate onto a field-path running parallel with the church wall. Follow the path through several kissing gates until it reaches the road at Bryers Fold. Turn right, walk along the road for a short distance (special care needed at the bend) and then turn right into a road signed to 'Cunsey'. Continue to the bottom of the hill; turn sharp left on to a track which becomes unsurfaced and follows the lake shore until the road is reached. Turn right and cross the road to the National Trust car park. For the ferry retrace the route taken at the start of the walk.

The Lakeshore

Length of walk: 5 miles
Start/finish: Ash Landing, 1/4 mile from the Ferry House Pier of the Windermere Ferry. There is a small National Trust car park opposite the start. At peak times this may fill early, so park at Ferry Nab car park, cross by the ferry and walk to the starting point (see walk 5).
Terrain: Generally on good tracks through woodland and by the lakeshore but a few sections can be muddy after heavy rain. Short distances on quiet roads.

The walk starts almost opposite the National Trust car park at Ash Landing. At a sharp bend in the road by the lakeshore look for a track with a small sign indicating 'Ash Landing Nature Reserve'. Follow this track for the next 300m along the lakeside. The entrance to the Nature Reserve is on the right just a few metres along the path and at most times of the year it has much of interest to see. A walk round the Reserve will add about half a mile to the total distance. Return to the shore path.

When the path by the lake shore swings to the right follow the drive up to the road. (This is a private road but a permissive footpath). Turn left along the road and, with woodlands on both sides, follow it for the next half mile noting the fine group of trees in the grounds of the house at Fellborough. At the end of the wooded area look for a footpath sign on the left leading back to the lakeshore across a field full of meadow flowers at mid-summer.

Rejoin the lakeshore path and follow it for the next three quarters of a mile to Rawlinson Nab. This is a delightful, easy stroll with meadows on the one hand and the lake on the other. At the beginning of this section Storrs Temple may be seen on the opposite shore. This stands out in the lake at the end of a short causeway and was built in 1804 to commemorate the victories of four British Admirals – Nelson, Blake, Duncan and St. Vincent. It is a unique monument in the Lake District. The fringes of the lake have a lush and varied growth of reeds, rushes, irises and other water plants which provide shelter and nesting sites for many species of water bird. Do not disturb them.

The footbridge across Cunsey Beck is, in summer months, a good place to see some of the vast population of minnows which flourish in Windermere while, at almost any point along this path you may see swans, mallard, merganser, pochard, shelduck, coots, cormorants, goldeneye, and perhaps tufted duck and teal. Rawlinson Nab is a craggy promontory, once a prime viewing 'station' but now partly covered in trees. It is still a pretty spot with fine views along the lake and is provided with a good seat strategically placed for this purpose.

Continue along the path by the Nab until its lakeshore route comes to an end and it swings to the right along a wire fence to a complex double stile by an old barn. Over the stile turn right along the road and proceed carefully round several sharp bends for about 500m to Low Cunsey Farm. Directly opposite the farm buildings is a bridleway sign pointing into a rather gloomy forest of conifers. Follow this wide forest track for about 300m and then bear right – do not follow it straight ahead to a field gate – and then turn left when it comes to a signpost by Cunsey Beck. (Follow the yellow footpath arrow not the blue bridleway arrow).

On the left of the path are the ruins of a large building which looks like a derelict barn but which is, in fact, all that remains of a once famous iron forge, known to have existed here as early as 1623, It became more important when an iron furnace was established lower down the beck near the lake in 1711 to smelt ore brought by water. The iron was then taken up to the forge which was powered by mill-wheels driven by the waters of Cunsey Beck. (The furnace buildings later became a bobbin mill and are now a joiner's workshop).

Continue along the track until it suddenly ends. Do not go through the gate but go forward along a narrow path – muddy after rain – by a plantation of mixed woodland with a deer fence on the left. This leads in just under half a mile to a stile and a road. Turn right along the road – which is fairly quiet but still has traffic – and in 250m come to a junction by Eel House and Cottage. Turn right here to Eel Bridge. From the bridge continue along the road for another 350m to a footpath sign on the right pointing to Far Sawrey. There is a good, distant view of the Langdale Pikes from this stile.

Just before the stile there is an unusual road sign warning motorists of toads crossing the road ahead. The 'toad' is often covered up outside the spawning season. Over the stile the path climbs fairly steeply

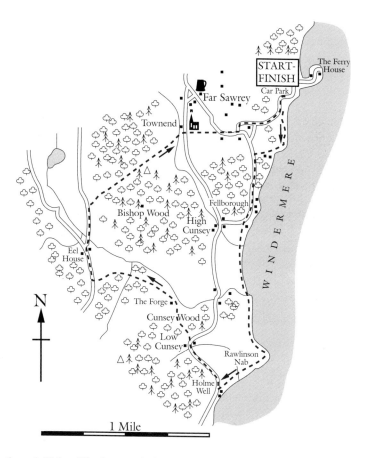

through Bishop Wood – a typical mixed woodland with many tree and shrub species and home to a variety of mammals. At the top of the wood a stile leads into pastures: cross to a gate and stile, go through the next gate and then straight ahead along a terraced path to a kissing gate by the road.

Turn left and then almost immediately right on to a field path close by the church. Follow this path up the fields through several kissing gates to reach the road at Bryers Fold. Turn right along the road for a very short distance –taking care at the bend – and then take an off-road footpath down to the National Trust car park, crossing the road once halfway down the hill. (If you came by ferry walk along the road back to the pier).

The Winster Valley

Length of walk: The route of this walk forms a figure-of-eight. The total distance is 5 miles but it may be covered as two separate walks of about 2½ miles each.

Start/finish: Either by Winster Church or on the roadside near Ghyll Head Reservoir. To reach the church take the A5074 Lyth Valley road for some 2½ miles from Bowness to the Brown Horse Inn; turn right by the inn; the church is on the left about 500m along this lane. Park near the church. To reach Ghyll Head Reservoir take the A592 Newby Bridge road for about 2½ miles from Bowness; turn left along a lane to Ghyll Head. A number of spaces will be found along the roadside above the reservoir and beyond.

Terrain: The route is along good tracks, field paths, woodland drives and some quiet stretches of Tarmac.

The Winster valley is a gentle landscape of woods, meadows, rocky knolls, fast-flowing streams and scattered white-washed houses, cottages and farms. The route is described with a starting point on the Ghyll Head road – Point A on the map. If the start is made from the church – Point B on the map – pick up the story at the place indicated in the text.

Proceed to a wide gateway on the left of the Ghyll Head road about 300m beyond the southern end of the reservoir. Go through this to join a good track with open country on the left and a wall on the right, continue past a tarn on the left. Pass by a gloomy driveway on the right and follow the track along the edge of the wood for another 300m. Look for a gate on the right – no signpost – leading into a lane, formerly a surfaced roadway, which is a private road but a public footpath going down directly to Winster House. Follow this round to the front of the house.

As you pass by note the dovecot built into the archway leading into the stable courtyard. From Winster House walk down the Tarmac driveway passing the medieval manor house of Birket Houses over to the left. At the end of the drive cross the River Winster and pass by the Old Vicarage on the right. Built into the gate-pillar is a coat-of-arms showing three scallops and a group of

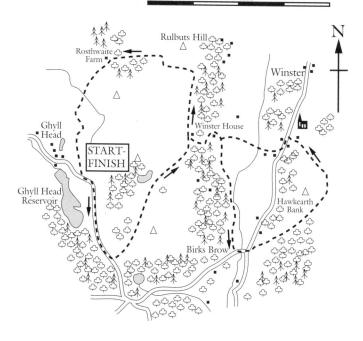

1 Mile

foxes. Continue forward for another 100m to a T-junction; turn left here to Bryan Houses, two 17th century houses, nestling in a hollow on the left.

Note: If the walk is started from Winster Church follow the directions from this point – marked B on the map. Walk along the lane from the church for 200m.

Directly opposite Bryan Houses Cottage a bridleway is signposted to Crag Lane and the A5074. Follow this but in about 50m fork right where a footpath sign points to Hawkearth Moss. A grassy track beyond the gate has occasional waymarks and leads in 400m to a footpath sign by a spring. Take the path to Roper Ford, a narrow path winding among gorse bushes down to a ladder stile over a wall in about 200m. Over the stile an occasionally indistinct path follows the wall on the left by mixed woodland, keeping close to the wall all the way for the next 500m, crossing one more ladder stile about half-way.

At the end of the path cross over a stone stile and in 25m cross straight over the road to Roper Ford. This is a pleasant spot with a stone footbridge over the River Winster. About 50m beyond the bridge follow a footpath sign to the right with a wood on the left and a wall on the right. Go through a gate and in about 100m note where the path forks – almost in line with a footbridge over the river on the right.

On the terraced track up on the left is a good example of the lime-kilns which were built throughout this district 200 years ago to burn the local limestone with peat or charcoal to create lime for fertilising the fields. Take the path straight ahead across the fields below the kiln, passing through gaps in the walls. Lowhouse Beck is crossed by the last wall – either by stepping, jumping or splashing, according to recent rains – and the path then bears slightly left up to the corner of a wood. Go through a gate here to join a grassy path which soon emerges by a kissing gate on to the drive in front of Winster House.

Turn left up the drive and retrace the route walked earlier – past the great barn, with its archway and dovecot, and up through the wood to a gate to rejoin the track on which the walk began. This section will, of course, be 'new' to those who started at Winster Church, but, wherever the walk was started, everyone should turn right here. Follow the track forward for about 500m, with the wall at first on the right and then, after a gate, on the left. This is fairly easy walking with views gradually opening over the valley towards Winster and to the wooded hills above Lake Windermere. At a junction of tracks take the left turn up the hill. Bear right just over the brow and go down to a gate which gives access to Spring Wood, a carpet of bluebells in May.

At the end of the wood is Rosthwaite Farm, now a stud for high-class horses. Turn left by the pond. Go through the gate at the end of the farm enclosure and continue along the track for another 150m down into a hollow where a footpath sign indicates the route straight ahead to Ghyll Head Road. The track now rises gently through a landscape of open, rough grazing pleasantly adorned with shrubs and some fine trees, and with a widening view.

300m from the signpost look for a lone oak tree with a footpath sign close by, again pointing the way to Ghyll Head Road. This is the route to follow but before doing so it is worth making a diversion to the top of Rosthwaite Heights, the small hill on the right. The view from here is quite splendid.

Return to the lone oak and go forward the short distance to the stile at the edge of the wood straight ahead. In about 100m the path divides at kissing gates. The path straight ahead goes over duckboards; take the alternative path through the kissing gate on the right and follow an interesting path through National Park Access Land among a variety of trees. A view over Ghyll Head Reservoir opens up towards the end of the path. Join the road and turn left. To complete the circuit follow the road for about half a mile to the wide gateway on the left – marked A on the map.

If returning to the church follow the directions given at the beginning – as far as Bryan Houses. The church is 200m straight ahead from here.

C. M. Lakenwood.

Underbarrow Scar

Length of walk: 5 miles.
Start/finish: The National Park car park on the Underbarrow road two miles west of Kendal. Look for a sign to the car park on the right of the road immediately over the brow of the hill.
Terrain: There is a short climb at the start but otherwise this is an easy route on limestone which gives a mainly dry surface.

A short distance beyond the urban limits of Kendal is open limestone country and a spectacular escarpment known as Underbarrow Scar and Scout Scar. This is an almost vertical cliff left when ice-age glaciers and floodwaters gouged out the Lyth Valley which lies hundreds of feet below. The valley is now a quiet pastoral scene famous for its springtime display of damson blossom but beautiful at any time. From the walk along the scar there are panoramic views in all directions. To the north and west an impressive array of fells; to the south the wide sweep of Morecambe Bay and the estuary of the River Kent; to the north and east a fine prospect of the High Street fells, the Whinfell range, the Howgills and the distant Pennines.

Cross the road by the car park – care is needed here – turn right and in a very few paces go through an iron gate on the left. Ignore the main path to the right just inside the gate (this is the return route) and take the smaller path straight ahead. Follow this up the slope as it winds its way among the heather and a variety of bushes. In about half a mile pass through a broken wall and immediately beyond this is the large stone trig point which at 229m (760ft) marks the summit.

There are several paths ahead from this point; almost any one may be chosen but do not veer too far to the right and aim for the corner of the wall straight ahead. This is the boundary of the National Trust property of Helsington Barrows. Follow the now clear path alongside the wall for a good half mile to a gate in the wall with a National Trust sign just inside. Go through this gate and follow a broad grassy track down to the road. Turn right down the road for a very short distance and take a wide track on the left over a cattle grid. A few minutes walk leads to St John's Church, Helsington. It is not an ancient church with a long history – it dates from 1726 – but it stands on one of the most delectable sites of any church in the country. High above the

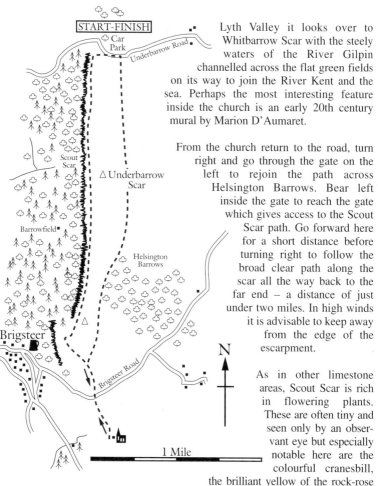

Lyth Valley it looks over to Whitbarrow Scar with the steely waters of the River Gilpin channelled across the flat green fields on its way to join the River Kent and the sea. Perhaps the most interesting feature inside the church is an early 20th century mural by Marion D'Aumaret.

From the church return to the road, turn right and go through the gate on the left to rejoin the path across Helsington Barrows. Bear left inside the gate to reach the gate which gives access to the Scout Scar path. Go forward here for a short distance before turning right to follow the broad clear path along the scar all the way back to the far end – a distance of just under two miles. In high winds it is advisable to keep away from the edge of the escarpment.

As in other limestone areas, Scout Scar is rich in flowering plants. These are often tiny and seen only by an observant eye but especially notable here are the colourful cranesbill, the brilliant yellow of the rock-rose and the bright purples of several varieties of orchid.

Towards the end of the walk turn aside to pay a visit to 'The Mushroom'. a raised metal shelter surmounted by a dome with a diagram which identifies the names of most of the surrounding fells. At the end of the scar the path turns right down a well-worn path to return to the road. Turn right. Cross the road to return to the car park.

Stott Park Bobbin Mill

Length of walk: 2¹/₂ miles (3¹/₂ with extension to Rusland Heights).
Start/finish: Stott Park Bobbin Mill, 1¹/₂ miles north of Newby Bridge,
near the foot of Lake Windermere. The mill has its own car parks.
Terrain: An undemanding climb to High Dam on clear paths.

This walk may be completed by making the return journey to Bowness by lake steamer from Lakeside (for all but the driver of the car!). A trip on the steam railway to Haverthwaite may also be included. The quay, the station and a car park are on the same site at Lakeside. A regular service is provided from May to November and also at certain times in April. Services are less frequent in winter. Times should be checked: Tel. 01539 31188.

The walk starts at Low Stott Park bobbin mill and a visit to the mill is recommended either at the beginning or the end of the walk. Stott Park bobbin mill opened in 1835 and worked continuously until 1971. Millions of bobbins were produced here for the Lancashire cotton industry, using coppice poles from the woodlands of South Lakeland. The mill has been fully restored and is now a working museum in the care of English Heritage. The whole process of bobbin manufacture is demonstrated using the original belt-driven machinery. Power to drive the machinery was until the 1850s provided by a waterwheel, 32ft in diameter, driven by the waters from Low Dam and High Dam which are visited on this walk. The mill is open every day between April 1 and October 31. Admission charge.

From the upper car park behind the mill cross the road to an off-road footpath signed to High Dam. Follow this to its end by the roadside in about 400m. Cross the road, turn left and in about 100m turn right by a signpost to High Dam. This road soon becomes a wide track passing by a small car park and on to a gate giving access to woodland. Follow a good track upwards bearing right at a fork, and noting the various tree species and the many plants and flowers (in season) on the woodland floor. In about half a mile the waters of Low Dam will be seen through the trees on the left, a shady, tranquil spot. A short distance beyond this is High Dam, one of the most attractive tarns in the Lake District, set among rocky knolls, heather-covered hillsides, a fringe of mixed woodland and with a fine display of water lilies. Look out for the many water-birds which visit the tarn.

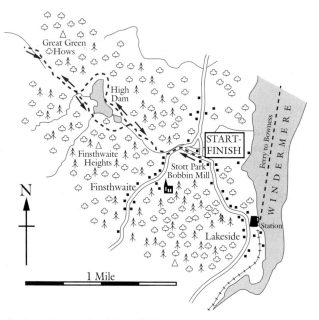

Cross the footbridge to the right and follow the path along the water's edge. This is a delightful place to linger before continuing round the tarn along a path fragrant with bog myrtle, colourful with many flowers and alive with bees and butterflies. Keep to the path round the tarn. It soon rises to a higher level to give clear views across the water. Eventually, where the shoreline turns near the end of a wall, a footpath sign points to the right to Rusland. The route may be extended here by a visit to Rusland Heights, a half-mile walk up to open moorland with extensive views over the Vale of Rusland, one of Lakeland's most peaceful and unspoilt valleys. Return to High Dam by the same route and rejoin the track along the tarn to the dam at its southern end. Cross the dam wall to rejoin the path back down to the right all the way back to the mill.

If, at this point, it is decided that some of the party would like to complete the expedition by taking the Lake Steamer (no vehicles) to Bowness proceed by car to Lakeside, about half a mile along the road towards Newby Bridge. This is a busy road: walking is not recommended especially with children. At Lakeside are the quay and railway station and a booking office where all arrangements may be made for tickets for both the Lake Steamer and the short trip by steam train to Haverthwaite and back to Lakeside. The 3½ mile railway is all that remains of a branch line of the Furness Railway.

Gummer's How

Length of walk: 1¹/₂ miles.
Start/finish: A minor road runs from the A592 Bowness to Newby Bridge road at Fell Foot signposted to Bowland Bridge. This climbs steeply and just before the top of the hill a car park is hidden among the trees on the right. The walk starts here.
Terrain: Easy level paths at first and a narrow rocky path to the summit. The descent is initially steep and rocky but, with reasonable care, it is not difficult or dangerous.

Gummer's How is 1053ft (321m) in height and is a prominent feature in the landscape near the foot of Lake Windermere. It is the highest point for some distance round the lake and so commands a famous view. This is a short walk but it is also the only real fell-walk in the book and, miniature though it may be, the ascent to and the descent from the summit need care. The reward is great for so little effort. A short path leads from the car park through the wood to the road. Cross the road to a gate and footpath sign. Beyond the gate a clear, level path leads directly towards Gummer's How, passing by woodland and open scrubland but in about 400m the terrain becomes rougher as the path begins to climb.

Near the base of the climb it is better not to take the direct route to the summit but to follow a path to the left which circles round the fell and approaches the top from the other side. This route has the advantage of a grandstand view of the lake: it is also much less steep. The summit is marked by an Ordnance Survey triangulation cairn. There are many pleasant places to sit to admire the spectacular view.

The dominant feature is the lake itself which can be seen for much of its length. It is possible to pinpoint many of the places visited on these walks: High Dam, Rawlinson Nab, the ferry, Orrest Head and the Vale of Winster. On the further horizons are Black Combe far away to the west, the monument on Hoad Hill near Ulverston, Coniston Old Man, Scafell Pike, Wetherlam, the Langdale Pikes; and the mountains

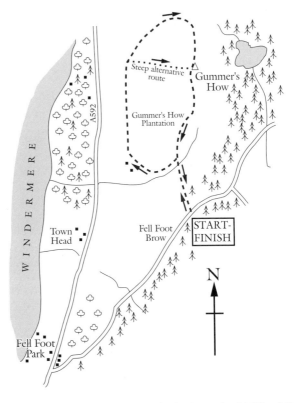

of the Helvellyn range clustered close together in the north with Wansfell and Red Screes. Towards the north-east is the dark ridge of the High Street fells while twenty miles to the east lie the Howgills and beyond that again is the long, blue ridge of the distant Pennines. Southwards, and much nearer, are the estuaries of the Rivers Kent and Leven and the sands of Morecambe Bay. At your feet, facing along the lake, is the land of the Swallows and Amazons. Descend by the steep, rocky path directly down from the summit. Care is needed at certain difficult points. Return to the car park by the same route.

This walk can be combined with a visit to the National Trust property 'Fell Foot Park and Garden' on the shore of Windermere near the A592 at the bottom of Gummer's How road. Fell Foot was part of a Victorian estate with extensive lakeside lawns and gardens and it is now being restored by the National Trust.